CATERPILLAR GIRL

poems by

Meredith Heller

Finishing Line Press
Georgetown, Kentucky

CATERPILLAR GIRL

ACKNOWLEDGMENTS

To California Wilderness—
my muse, my healer, my joy

Publisher: Leah Huete de Maines
Editor: Christen Kincaid
Cover Art: ruthevansart.com; Ruth Evans
Author Photo: Natalie Keshlear
Cover Design: Elizabeth Maines McCleavy

Order online: www.finishinglinepress.com
also available on amazon.com

Author inquiries and mail orders:
Finishing Line Press
PO Box 1626
Georgetown, Kentucky 40324
USA

Contents

We can never be born enough.
—e. e. cummings

On Earth, everyone loved butterflies,
but I trusted the caterpillars more. I trusted
the ones who knew they were not done growing.
—Andrea Gibson

Caterpillar Girl

Yuba River, Nevada City, CA

She is one of those
young women
with a sunflower face
a heart full of honey
eyes scooped
from the river.

She swings
through her days
in a red silk slip
that kisses her knees
plunges at the neck
revealing the soft curve
of her breast.

And there along the edge
of her hem, a caterpillar
suddenly prehistoric
thick as your thumb
with red-tipped horns
crawling up her dress.

Oh! She yelps not sure yet
if she feels afraid or blessed
when her ocean-eyed lover asks,
scared? Nah, she laughs
and settles in
curious and content.

We chit-chat
about camping and traveling
and the possibility of Yosemite
and all the while
this caterpillar climbs,
with its multitude

of wrought-iron legs
up her body
finally nestling
in the hair
atop her head.

We joke about it
spinning a cocoon
that will hang
from her ear
like a silken dangle.

She'll sleep sitting up
for weeks in service
to its birthing
and one fine day
it will emerge.

After having turned to goo
melting and metabolizing
each and every molecule
into imaginal cells
that dream themselves anew
winged and wild
and ready
to fly.

Tahoe

Lake Tahoe, Sierra Nevada Mountains, CA

When I say the word blue
there's no way you can know
what I mean. It's like another planet.
My belly flipflops;
water becomes sky becomes water,
and still, you cannot fathom it.
Unless you're sitting here beside me
on this pile of moon rocks
at the edge of the world.
Your bones turning to liquid,
your smile etched by sunlight,
your skin throwing sparks, as you melt
into a blue—vaster, clearer, deeper
than any blue or any other thing
you have ever known.
And here, at the rim of this basin of glory,
you feel your own voice catch in your throat
and you raise the rigging of your heart
and set sail for this blue, bluest, blueing.

Bloomers

Yuba River, Nevada City, CA

I washed each pair
with Dr Bronner's
lavender castile soap
in a bucket
with river water.

I scrubbed
I swished
I made sure
there were lots
of bubbles.

I rinsed their thin skins
thoroughly wringing out
the old ghosts
from their cotton crotches
and lace trim.

I hung each frillery
on a length of string
I'd strung between two trees
bordering my campsite.

Each pair draped gingerly
over the line—
purple lace boy shorts
tiger-striped bikini
black & white tie-dye hipster
hot pink thong.

I have to admit,
they were beautiful creatures,
each one dangling there
swinging its legs

nickering its own little story
after having nestled
my most intimate parts.

I sit on the big rock
to admire my clean tribe
of dainties with a smile
on my face, and I think,
now this is my kind
of prayer flag.

Panty prayers
wind scribbling
dream flowers
across satin petals.

Incantations stained
into silken skin
my signature
inscribed in sighs.

The elements eating
away their karma
rejoicing their secrets
and their sins.

Tahquitz

Tahquitz Canyon, Palm Springs, CA

Tahquitz! You were the first shaman created by Mukat, the creator of all things, brought forth to help the Cahuilla People of the Agua Caliente Tribe.

But you turned bad, possessed by power and banished to a canyon in the San Jacinto Mountains where you live on, rumbling the range, haunting the night sky with your green fireball of fury.

Why not come sit here with me, beside this waterfall that gushes from the mouth of the rock face, and dive into its river of cold clarity until your pain loosens.

Come rest here with me in the shadow of this cave and cool your anger in the presence of the Grandfather Stones until their chanting enters your blood and their eyes absorb your betrayal.

~

Hey Tahquitz! I found your heart. Hidden in a tangle of rotting leaves. Small and dark and petrified. I pulled it out and set it atop a granite boulder. I asked the Sun to eat away its envy.

I walked home through spring blooms of star-vine and golden head, stopping to lay my cheek against warm rock spires glowing rubescent in the afternoon sun, their veins full of quartz.

I thought maybe I'd go back in a week or two to check on your heart, but if you get there before I do, hold it in your hands until you remember the goodness in you, the goodness in everything.

Eclipse

Joshua Tree, CA

*To the white lizard who crossed my path on the eve of
the lunar eclipse*

A zigzag of lightning
across black asphalt
an emissary
from tomorrow's
terracotta moon
full lunar eclipse—
      an invitation
from the shadowlands
to dig in the dirt
touch the bones
of what we've buried
      yes, we will all go dark
for an hour or so
dissolve into dusk
climb inside ourselves
to glimpse the backside
of our heart
      and if we're not swallowed
alive by the hungry creature
who resides there
we'll open our collective eye
and bloom like a penumbra
that ghost that burns
      the lip of the moon
on a hot summer night
in the desert
I had to sit a long time
in stillness to understand
      the texture of your skin
and when I look closely enough
I begin to see myself
reflected, scale upon scale
shifting with the light, each eye

roving independently
on its own axis
        rubiking its own riddle
like an ouroboros
consuming itself
in cyclical renewal.

Origami Birds

Yuba River, Nevada City, CA

she's got a silver tongue
  and tinsel twirled hair

skin burnished copper
  as she camps beside the river

spinning stories
  with her paper and pen

like origami birds
  that she folds in thirds

and gives them
  a reason to fly.

Datura Flowers

Joshua Tree, CA

I ran into Don Juan today
picking datura flowers
along the trail
with careful fingers
he reached inside
the white trumpets
of their throats
and pulled out
the magic seeds.

Ravens drew circles
in the sky above
marking the temenos
while the good doctor
gathered medicine
for the people.

He chanted over the seeds
asking them to oil
the rusty hinges
and swing open
the ancient doors
between worlds.

He asked the seeds
to place the key
in our own hands
so we can learn to turn it
as the cosmos turns
as we ourselves turn and tremble
here on the lip
of the universe.

Don Juan raised himself up
brushing dirt from his knees
a smile spreading across

his desert clay face
he held out his handful of seeds
each luminescent bead singing
inviting us to take our place
as magic makers
in this great mystery.

Insect Lady

Madelyn Helling Library, Nevada City, CA

Today at the library, I met the insect lady.
It wasn't that she was an insect exactly
but she was wearing this white silk blouse
covered completely with pictures of insects.

When you think about it, even the silk,
was spun from worms
which would've morphed into moths
had they not shucked their cocoons.

The shirt was a marvel, buttoned up high
with tiny pearlescent moon buttons
offsetting her brown hair
coifed in 1940s finger waves
oval-framed glasses
perched on her buttercup nose,
archetypal librarian.

And then she did something unexpected and wonderful—
when the library didn't have the book I wanted
she ordered it for me from that mega-monopoly
that sells everything we absolutely do not need.

As I turned to go
bubbling my thanks
I glimpsed black
tentacles tattooed
along her clavicles
and I remembered—

Beneath the persona, no matter
which way a person's mask
twists to catch the light,
under the surface

under the skin
is where
the true story
is written.

Bone Song

Thank you!
For the crystalline minerals
you donated to fill the blackhole
of sorrow that opened
when I shattered
my wrist.

I want you to know
that your calcite cathedrals
did not go to waste
but seeded my bones
to grow new gardens
so I can play guitar again
and sing.

And though my hand will never
be what it once was
I have learned a new way
the left-hand path
that allows me
to hold myself
and others
with greater patience
and kindness.

So, thank you—
for these two small bone-ghosts
grafted onto the branch
of my right radius.

Sure, I wonder who you were—
Did you too play guitar?
Did you did talk with your hands?
Was there someone you loved to touch?

And what now, that part of you
lives inside of me?
Do your circadian rhythms
influence my melodies?

Is that you chanting beside me
as I string bracelets
pushing a prayer
through each tiny bead,
my hand steady as steel.

Gratitude is the deepest
way I know how to pray,
this, and my song.

I sit with my guitar
fingers strumming
metal strings ringing
and I know
that together
we are greater
than the sum
of our bones.

Morning Harvest
Ring Mountain, Marin County, CA

i
Fog bank
saves morning gold
builds fortune of light
yields afternoon profit
scatters shares at dusk
across the bay.

ii
Spring sings
with a tremolo
down the serpentine
as leaf boats
of fern and raspberry
float and swivel
unbridled.

iii
Red bellied snake
thick as an artery
conduit
from heart
to limb.

iv
Red tailed hawk
sun singing
your wing.

v
Climbing the steep hill
feet digging in earth
legs swinging as I crest
breath bellowing
body splitting open
and suddenly,
I am.

vi
Granite beings
jag the sky
tipped golden
and green with lichen
nook gathered
dew supped
ridge wrinkled
we grow in circles
spreading like water.

vii
I lean in
and find
we are
kin.

viii
Driftwood bones
ghost songs in A minor
syllables rusting
in desire's grove.

Vultures circling overhead
Have at it!
I scream.

Peck
my bones
clean.

ix
I could just
let go
and roll
down
this hill

caked in mud
clothed in dry grass
washed by wind
tattooed by sunlight.

x
Come spring
the yellow lily
wild and hearty
as a weed.

The Art Studio

Tennessee Valley, Mill Valley, CA

In the art studio
at the edge of the world
where the turquoise ocean tumbles

Swallowtail butterflies
dance
with their shadows

We found wildflowers
eons of stone
a renegade apple tree

We sat huddled together
a campfire
of two souls

Pebbles, waves, clouds, hills
weaving us into their song
of belonging

This life calls us home
crawling on our knees
till we surrender to the soil

Turn our wounds into compost
crack the husk of our heart
plant it in the dark unknown

Full moon gathered herself
turning with the tide
as we walked back into the world

Each of us a lighthouse
taller and brighter
than before.

Feast

Roy's Redwoods, San Geronimo Valley, CA

Clasp
your hands
together
in front of you
as you walk
this trail
of redwoods
high
on the scent
of cedar
bow
to the ferns
to your first trillium
gather
all this beauty
into the bowl
of your heart
for later
when you're hungry
and empty
when you forget
the feast of nature
how it quenches
your every
longing
touches
your every wound
making it
open
and bleed,
open
and bloom.

Wild Blackberries

Abbotts Lagoon, Point Reyes, CA

Along the trail,
we come upon them
and suddenly it all makes sense–

This wild berry
tiny dark heart
beating with joy.

Fingers purpled
from picking and popping
them into my mouth

And yours
two and three at a time,
shamelessly.

I paint a war stripe
down the center
of your face.

Our smiles need no words
we are high on sun-slang
cracked open on summertime–

Laughter is another way
of praying.

My Body Is Earth

My feet redwood groves, living in circles of sisters
tall and lean, rooted in rhythm, reaching for sunlight.

My calves the heathered moors of Scottish highlands
lonely drone of bagpipes and Celtic songs of love and loss.

My knees the Sierra Mountain Range pumping hills and valleys
amongst bobcat and big horned sheep and spring wildflowers.

My thighs thousands of miles of Australian desert. Dancing
songlines in the dreamtime of Earth, drumbeat of primal
awakening: animal, instinct, desire.

My sex the warm Mediterranean Sea, underwater caves where
light is birthed from hot springs at low tide on full moon in
tunnels dug by ebb and flow.

My gut underbelly of moist mycelium. Undersong, tangled
and twisted, squeezing through subterranean grottos where
bacteria make their music in the dark.

My heart Hawaii. Whales breaching. Night blooming cereus.
Volcano of molten love, erupting without apology in fountains
of fire; quenching Pele's burning need.

My brain the Amazon Rainforest. Green, growing, cacophony
of poetry pulsing. A meteor singes the night sky, and I know
I am part of this glorious mystery.

My voice a river of song. The Yuba, who holds me against
her body like a summer lover, who breaks open in spring
singing her wild truth, clearing the way for new life.

My Body is Earth.

Tomales Bay
Point Reyes, CA

Indian summer day
we stop for oysters
at Nick's Cove.

I play the piano
in the boat shack
at the end of the dock.

The water
plays prism
with the light.

I strip down
nude
dive in.

Warm silky water
touches me everywhere
I ache to be known.

I twist and twirl
a creature
one with the water.

Sun-stars sluice my skin
sing my cells
I float.

When I finally emerge
on the sandy cove
you're waiting for me.

Watching, like you've just seen
something wild and holy
being born.

Meredith Heller is a poet, nature lover, educator, and author of *Write a Poem, Save Your Life, Writing by Heart*, and three poetry collections. She leads workshops at schools, women's prisons, creativity & wellness retreats, and online. Her passion is empowering people to believe in themselves, trust their creative instincts, tap their wild wisdom, and express their truth. She lives in Northern California. Join her for a workshop and express the wild beauty of your heart.
www.MeredithHeller.com

www.ingramcontent.com/pod-product-compliance
Lightning Source LLC
Chambersburg PA
CBHW022101080426
42734CB00009B/1445